# How to Get Your
# Prayers
# Answered

# How to Get Your

# Prayers

# Answered

by Rabbi Irwin Katsof
(co-author of *Powerful Prayers* with Larry King)

Frederick Fell Publishers, Inc.
Hollywood, FL

**Library of Congress Cataloging-in-Publication Data**
Katsof, Irwin, 1955-
    How to get your prayers answered  /  by Rabbi Irwin Katsof.
        p.   cm.
    ISBN 0-88391-009-8
    1. Prayer - Judaism. 2. God (Judaism) I. Title.

                                                    CIP
    BM669 .K37 2000                            99-043325


Interior Design by Vicki Heil
10 9 8 7 6 5 4 3 2

# Words of Praise...

"Some books have the awesome power to change your life.... for certain this is one. Simply the clearest, static free, open line to the Divine ever written. Thank you Rabbi Katsof. Our prayers have indeed been answered!"

—**Harvey Mackay**, author of *Swim With the Sharks* and *Pushing the Envelope*

"In this wonderful new book about prayer, Rabbi Katsof opens the door to a deeper, more practical, more penetrating experience of God."

—**Marianne Williamson**, author of
*A Return to Love: Reflections on the Principles of a Course in Miracles*

"An important book that shows us, in practical terms, how to reach out to God and make our prayer more real."

—**Barbara DeAngelis, Ph.D.**, author of
*Secrets About Life Every Woman Should Know*

"Rabbi Katsof has given us a book on prayer which is filled with insight and wisdom—a valuable resource."

—**Dr. Jeane J. Kirkpatrick**, former U.S. ambassador

"Like a puzzle which is only complete by filling in all the pieces, this book puts prayer into a lovely, balanced, vibrant, and most accessible perspective."

—**Rabbi Reuven P. Bulka**, radio talk show host

"Anyone who is or who wants to be a believer, Jew or gentile, Muslim or Scientologist, Dodger or Giant fan, should find something in *Prayers* by Rabbi Irwin Katsof."

—**Elliott Gould**, actor

"This book is an enormous source of wisdom, insight and comfort for me. It confirms my personal belief in the Power of Prayer!"

—**Florence Henderson**, actress

"This is a valuable, moving, clearly written and wonderfully accessible book. Whether you are a religious scholar or a hopeful beginner, anyone can benefit from its profound (but common sense) recommendations."

—**Michael Medved**, film editor for the *New York Post*

"This little book speaks to us on many levels and shines with wisdom. I love it."

—**Mortimer Zuckerman**, chairman of Boston Properties

In memory of my beloved
parents who gave me the gift of life...

Sara Rifkah bas Yosef
Shirley Katsof
and
Avraham ben Yaakov Zvi
Albert Katsof

❦

May the growth people achieve through this book be
a tribute to their memory. May the growth people
attain through this book elevate the souls of my
parents closer to the Source of all growth.

# Acknowledgements

I would like to thank my teacher, Rabbi Noah Weinberg, founder and dean of Aish HaTorah. Rabbi Weinberg has probably reconnected more people to the awareness that God loves them and only wants their good than anyone else alive today. If not for him, I would not be who I am today. He gave me my relationship with God. I learned from him "how to get your prayers answered." I am merely the conduit for his teachings.

I want to thank Uriela Obst—a truly humble and extremely talented human being. Without her, this project would never have come to fruition. She edited the manuscript and pulled this whole book together.

To my absolutely amazing staff: Elise Ansky, Ann Hamada, Robin Lerner, Randy Rosen, Daniela Sztulwark, and Tiffany Tinson. They are all winners! They allow me to accomplish all that I do. It would be impossible to do so many different projects without their tremendous co-ordination of all the details.

To my many associates at Aish HaTorah who contributed their ideas—Rabbi Ari Kahn, Rabbi Eric Coopersmith, Rabbi Motty Berger, Rabbi Tom Meyer, Rabbi Zelig Pliskin, Rabbi Shmuel Silinsky, and Rabbi Steve Baars—thank you for your help, support and brilliant insights.

Thank you, as well, to Rabbi Nechemia Coopersmith, director of the Aish HaTorah International Research & Development department, for his guidance and support.

Thank you to my in-laws, Neale and Barbara Rosenthal, for their support and encouragement, for critical reading of the manuscript and for constructive suggestions throughout this book, as well as for my prior book, *Powerful Prayers*. You are my greatest fans and best spokespersons.

To my beautiful children, who are certainly my prayers answered. They always want to be mentioned in my books. Okay, here is your mention—Batya, Aaron, Yaakov, Simcha, Bracha, Sholom, and Sara. You are the greatest. You give me so much pleasure. Thank God for each of you.

To my wife, Judy, thank you for being my partner. You have taught me so much about life and what it means to be a decent human being. You keep me grounded through all the ups and downs. I could not do all this without your constant support, love and understanding. Thank you.

# Introduction

Imagine the following scenario: You live in a small town in Midwestern America, but life is not all peaches and cream. There is a large pothole in front of your house, and for the last four months the local municipality has ignored your requests to have it fixed. Finally, in an act of utter frustration, you call the White House. You are so furious that when the operator answers, you demand to speak to the president.

To your amazement, the president gets on the line! You stammer a bit, but you manage to explain your problem. The president doesn't say anything, and you are so flustered that you hang up the phone. You don't expect anything to be done about it anyway.

But the next morning, you look out your window and, lo and behold, there is a phalanx of green trucks on your street. The Army Corps of Engineers is busy at work fixing your road. The president of the United States took your request seriously and sent in the troops to help!

This is what it means to have your prayers answered.

Except that God is infinitely more powerful than the president of the United States. God is the Creator of the Universe, the Designer of the Cosmos, the Infinite Genius Who Created Every Molecule on Earth, and He can do a lot more than fill a pothole for you. God can alter the course of entire existence in order to answer your prayer.

And, believe it or not, it is a lot easier to get God on the line than the president. God is sitting by the phone actually waiting for you to call.

The problem is that most of us don't know how to go about "calling" God—either we don't quite understand Who we are calling, what number to dial, or what to say if by some chance we got through. So we don't try, we don't call. We don't understand that God is waiting for us—He wants a relationship with us.

This is the reason for this little how-to guide.

It came about in response to the many questions I received in connection with the publication of *Powerful Prayers: Conversations on Faith, Hope and the Human Spirit*, a book of interviews about spirituality with highly prominent and influential people, which I co-authored with CNN's Larry King. Even before that book hit the store shelves—when advance copies of the manuscript were being circulated—people were asking me for prayer "tips." If I could boil down what they wanted to know most of all, it would probably come down to this: "Okay rabbi, but how do you get your prayers answered?"

Surprising as it may seem, there is a way. I am not saying that it can happen overnight, but it's a lot easier than you'd think.

The user-friendly five-step formula I describe here, however, does come with a few prerequisites.

First, it takes some preparation. Therefore, I urge you to resist the impulse for a quick fix by flipping to the pages outlining the steps. Take the time to carefully read the explanatory sections and become acquainted with all the necessary concepts and definitions. For example, because you must know who it is that you are praying to, having a clear definition of God at the very outset is key. Another fundamental element is prayer itself—what it is and what it is not. In short, before you begin, you must understand clearly—in your mind and heart—what the experience of communicating with the Almighty is all about, and only then can you expect to reap the benefits.

Second, even though this is a short book and can be read in a couple short hours, I urge you to read slowly. It would be a good idea to read with a notepad by your side, so that you can jot down your thoughts as you go along. Ideally, I recommend you spread your reading of this material over several days, taking the time to ponder and internalize each of the five steps one by one.

Rest assured that everything presented here is based on the most authoritative religious book we have—the Bible. I can safely say that the ancient universal truths it imparts are relevant to people of all faiths. I have also relied on other ancient spiritual texts, in particular: the Talmud, a compilation of Jewish Oral Law that is considered an indispensable companion to the Bible; the Kabbalah, the mystical interpretation of the Bible; and other writings of Sages and Biblical commentators over the last two thousand years.

I hope this material proves as helpful in your spiritual journey as it has already been to many others. But most of all, I hope that, in rediscovering some very ancient but tried-and-true ways to come closer to God, you find that all your prayers are answered.

Rabbi Irwin Katsof
e-mail: myprayers@aol.com

# How To Get Your Prayers Answered

# In Five User-Friendly Steps

For most people the issue is not prayer. For most people the issue is God.

Unless you believe in a God Who hears you, you cannot pray.

Unfortunately, it seems to be politically correct these days to rationalize and intellectualize God. If you have bought into the idea that has gained popularity in some denominations—that God is good but not all-powerful— then you may well be having difficulty with prayer.

It's simple really. Once you've cut God down to your own size, you can no longer take God or prayer seriously. And I don't blame anyone who feels this way.

Unless you can address God like you mean it—and mean it because it is the Almighty you are talking to— then there is no point to praying.

# Who Is God Anyway?

❧

## "I am Who I am."

God to Moses, Exodus 3:14

G od is the name we give in the Western World to the most powerful being we know. That is why universally we call Him the Almighty. The Bible teaches that God is infinite. That is, God has no limitations of any kind that we could imagine. The Kabbalists call God "The Endless One."

The idea of an infinite God is hard for us to grasp with our finite minds, which are very much restricted by our limited way of knowing things through our five senses. Therefore, the Bible gives us some assistance. To begin with, it tells us that God is our Creator. God created our world and everything in it.

I was astonished to find out that until 1923—when Edwin Powell Hubbell made his startling discovery—astronomers thought that the Milky Way was the only galaxy in the Universe. Now we know that the Milky Way—a flat disk of about a hundred billion stars, almost a hundred thousand light years across—is but one of many billions of such galaxies extending billions of light years in all directions. That's what we know. What we don't know—and can scarcely imagine—is how much bigger it could be.

God created these seemingly endless galaxies. Indeed, God created all of the Universe. And that means that He is "bigger" than all that and beyond all that, which is what infinite means.

The Bible teaches us that besides being infinite, all-powerful and the creator of all existence, God is also both transcendent and immanent. These are lofty words, but what do they mean really? And how do they help us understand God?

Transcendent means that God is "out there." God exists outside of space and time, above and beyond our earthly concept of reality. Indeed, God is reality itself, and we exist in reality, in God. That is exactly why we say that while being transcendent, God is, at the very same time, immanent, which means God is "in here." God is with us, up-close and personal.

To underscore the closeness of the relationship, the Bible tells us that God is our parent. This is why—even though God runs the Universe—we have become fond of calling Him "Our Father in Heaven." Why "Our Father" and not "Our Mother?"

The Bible, Talmud and Kabbalah make it clear that God is neither a "He" nor a "She" and certainly not an "It." However, the Bible was originally written in Hebrew, which assigns masculine or feminine properties to all verbs. When God is proactive—"creates" the world and "forms" the first human being, for example—these action verbs are masculine and translators into English use the pronoun "He." When God is receptive, interactive or nurturing, God is given feminine characteristics. For example, the *Shechinah*, God's warm and loving presence, is always feminine.

The Sages teach that the presence of the *Shechinah* is most strongly felt during times of introspection when we examine our actions, are moved to ask forgiveness of those we might have hurt, and forgive those who hurt us. In the Hebrew calendar this time period is known as the month of Elul, which precedes the High Holy Days of Rosh Hashana and Yom Kippur.

A friend of mine, Miri, who had been single for many years, decided to take advantage of the unique opportunity for closeness with God that the month of Elul presents to pray that she should meet her soulmate. Miri, like many people, had somehow felt herself insignificant in the eyes of God and couldn't think of a reason why God should listen to her or answer her prayer, though she often prayed quite fervently for world peace, healing of the sick and other causes far removed from herself. Yet, hearing me speak about the fact that God is so close at this time, so loving, so receptive, she decided to take the plunge and spill out in words what she kept bottled up in her heart.

The day she started praying, she met the man whom she was clearly destined to marry. "The sky was so blue that day, and when I met Jake I felt like it was inches above our heads." It was the 10th of Elul and she naturally attached a great deal of significance to that date. Imagine her shock when, while leafing through the Bible a few months later, she came across a commentator's footnote regarding the 10th of Elul. It is believed that on that date, Noah opened the window of the ark, realizing that it had stopped raining and the waters of the great flood were receding.

Miri would say later, "It was like I, too, had opened a window in my heart to allow God into the most vulnerable part of me. And instantly, I got a response."

That is all that God wants from us—to be let into our lives, to be invited to sit and stay, like a close relative.

When we call God "Our Father," we relate to Him on a very intimate level that only a close family relationship would allow. Sometimes, when we want to remind ourselves of the immanent quality of God, without forgetting the transcendent aspect, we address Him as "Our Father, Our King."

He is the most powerful father and the wealthiest king that we can imagine. And because we are His children, He loves us unconditionally. There is nothing He doesn't want to give us and there is nothing He can't give us if He so chooses.

Underneath it all, on a subconscious level, we all realize this is true—we intuit that if we talk to God, He will respond in a loving way. That's why all people—even those who are not at all religious—at some time or another, will pray.

There's a well-known saying that "there are no atheists in a foxhole." It suggests that in time of danger and distress—when we feel like a soldier in a foxhole with the enemy advancing—even the most irreligious among us will call out "Dear God, get me out of this in one piece!" Or as one American soldier in Vietnam told the Associated Press: "A man does a lot of praying in an enemy prison." [*The Eyewitness History of the Vietnam War*, Ballantine Books: 1983]

At such times, what are you really saying? "Dear God: I know I've ignored You all these years and not appreciated all You have done for me, but I'm in trouble now, and I know You're the only One Who can help."

Implied in this plea is a deep-seated belief that God can help. And if you had ignored Him all your life until this moment of distress, then you must be assuming that God loves you. Why else would He pay attention to you now?

So even that atheist, who in a moment of trouble decides he has nothing to lose by praying, on some level intuits that the Biblical concept of God is true.

Since the Garden of Eden human beings have known that God is a loving and giving parent Who yearns for a relationship with us. There, God created a blissful world—Paradise—for the enjoyment of Adam and Eve. He gave them everything He possibly could, except a relationship with Him. A relationship, by its very nature, is a two-way street; each party has to choose it. Otherwise, it's not a relationship.

So Adam and Eve had to choose to have a relationship with God of their own free will. But they decided to compete with God rather than cooperate with Him, and a chance at a real relationship was lost. Ever since then we have been trying to find our way back, and God has been hoping we will.

God is a loving father, Who is always waiting for us to reestablish contact with Him, just as any good parent would be if his child had for some reason cut off relations.

Stella, one of my students, admitted to me that for many years she never prayed. She did not believe that God listened to prayers and she thought the exercise of talking into space at best silly and at worst offensive to an intelligent mind. Then one day, a very close friend of hers, a woman named Naomi, tearfully asked Stella if she would pray for her mother who was dying of cancer. Stella did not want to lie and said she would pray, so she braced herself to explain to her friend why she could not fill her request. But before Stella could do so, Naomi clarified what she had in mind. She had decided to have the entire Book of Psalms said for her mother and she had to find 150 people willing to read one psalm each. It had been an arduous task.

"But I—" Stella started to say.

"Please don't say no," Naomi pleaded, knowing her friend well enough to surmise what she was thinking. "I already have 138 people. I only need twelve more. Please, please say Psalm 139 for my mom."

Stella realized she could not hurt her friend at a time like this, and so she agreed.

She decided to get the reading over with as quickly as possible, and wincing a little, she opened the Book of Psalms. But, as her eyes fell on the opening lines, involuntary tears blurred the words:

*"Lord, you have searched me and You know me...*
*You understand how to draw me near to You from afar..."*

In a flash of insight, she understood that God had simply gotten tired of waiting for her to establish contact and had sent her a message via this beautiful prayer.

The next day Stella called Naomi and thanked her for the enormous gift she had given her. Naomi did not seem surprised. "Half a dozen people called to say the psalm I asked them to say for my mom turned out to be the very prayer they needed to be saying for themselves."

That was the start of a "beautiful friendship" with God for Stella. Today she says that prayer is a highlight of her day; this is when she feels connected, loved, looked after by a loving Father and an Almighty Creator Who so gently invited a relationship with her in the form of a friend's tearful request.

Stella's attitude toward God is not atypical. The most recent Gallup Poll shows that 90 percent of Americans pray on a weekly basis, and 75 percent pray daily. A surprising statistic. Much has been written about this phenomenon of late. A *Newsweek* magazine survey reported similar results but added an interesting twist. Even more surprising than the statistic was the testimony of God's love implied in the survey. The majority of the interviewed—and this amazingly included those who by their own admission generally ignored God—said that they'd had their prayers answered. No matter how these people treated God, when they finally broke down and prayed, God answered their prayers!

Can you imagine the implications of having your prayers answered? That means that the Creator of some hundred billion stars—each one bursting with the power of millions of atom bombs—took time out from running the Universe to listen to you and your concerns, and marshaled the awesome power at His disposal to grant your request. But, if God is, like the Bible says, all-powerful and all-loving, then you shouldn't be surprised. Of course, He'd do anything for His children. He loves us!

But how many of us pray with the expectation that our prayers will be answered?

There is a story told about three farmers who, during a period of drought, stand out in the field praying for rain. A man comes along and asks them what they are doing. "Praying for rain," they answer.

"Nah," the man says, "I don't think so."

"What?" The first farmer exclaims, insulted. "Don't you see we are down on our knees begging God?"

"Yes," says the second farmer, "we are putting our hearts into it."

"We are not asking for ourselves," the third farmer chimes in, "but for our families and our community."

"Hogwash, you are wasting your time," the man declares.

"Why do you say that?" they demand to know.

"Because, to get your prayers answered you have to believe that they will be, and you guys don't!"

"But we do!"

"Not really. If you did, you would have brought an umbrella."

To pray properly you have to believe that your prayers will be answered. Otherwise, you are always holding back, not really believing that God can make it happen. To get your prayers answered you have to believe in your heart of hearts that not only is God all-powerful—and can fulfill your every request—but that He loves you and that His love for you is infinite, therefore, He wants to fulfill your every request.

This brings us to the very first step for getting our prayers answered.

# Step One

I magine for a moment that you are a college student home for the holidays. Your father, who has been paying your $25,000 annual tuition, is taking you out to lunch when you remember that you have to make a quick phone call. "Dad," you say, "can I have a quarter?"

Now, for even a second, does it cross your mind that he might say no? Of course not. A quarter is an insignificant amount of money. Your father has already given you much, much more than that. And he loves you dearly. Why would he deny you such a small thing?

As strange as it seems, this illustration hints at the first step to getting your prayers answered—praying with an expectation of a positive result.

God is your Father in Heaven. How much richer is God than the father sending his child to Harvard? How much more loving? How much more giving? God has already given us life. Everything else is equivalent to a quarter in comparison. Nothing you could ask for could possibly make God any poorer, any less mighty. And God wants to give you more. You just need to accept God's love and gifts.

But strangely enough, a lot of people don't pray with that attitude. Some have the wrong idea about God as a punishing tyrant instead of the loving parent He is. Others believe that God is too "busy" taking care of the problems of the world and so they avoid asking, or they avoid praying altogether. Still other people consider themselves not important enough to take up God's attention. How can this be? An all-powerful God too busy? An all-loving God not paying attention to one of His children?

This kind of attitude, far from humble, can also be interpreted as being denigrating to God. By not expecting the best from God, you are either doubting God's capabilities or His willingness to give, which, in either case, is—to be honest—an insult.

But if you don't expect to be heard with loving and attentive ears by your Creator, and if you don't expect to get the best, God is not going to force anything on you. God won't invade your space.

So, to get your prayers answered, pray as if you mean it—knowing that God loves you and wants to give to you—fully expecting that all the best is coming your way.

# Summary of Step One:

# Pray Like You Expect Results

"When I look to the heavens
and I see the work of Your hand,
the moon and the stars which You have
created, I ask, 'What is man that
You remember him?
And what is the son of Adam that
You should care for him?'
You have made him little less
than divine, and You have crowned
him with honor and dignity."

King David Psalm 8

Now that you know who it is that you are praying to, and you have the right attitude, expecting to have your prayers answered, you can ask: How do I proceed? What prayers should I say? In what order?

There are so many definitions for prayer, but which one is correct?

Is prayer a conversation with God? If so, why does it feel so much like a monologue and not a dialogue? Can prayer be anything—a fleeting thought even—as long as it is heartfelt and sincere? Is there a better and worse way to pray?

# What Is Prayer?

❧

"Human prayer is the service of the spirit. Although people do not realize it, it involves the highest mysteries. For prayer splits through the atmosphere, through all firmaments, opens all doors and ascends on high."

*Zohar*, chief work of the Kabbalah

First and foremost, prayer is an expression of our relationship with God. What is that relationship?

God is our Father and we are His children. As such we are dependent on Him. Therefore, it is a relationship of dependency.

We are deluding ourselves if we think we are making it on our own, that God is not watching, not running the show. But if we choose to act that way, sometimes God lets us.

God gave us free will, and He generally keeps out of our lives until we acknowledge the relationship. We learn this from the opening sentences of the Bible: *"This is the history of the heavens and the earth when they were created, on the day the Lord God made earth and heaven. All the plants of the field were at this time in the ground and all the vegetation of the field had not yet sprouted for the Lord God had not brought rain upon the earth as there was no human being to work the soil."* [Genesis 2:4-5]

Rashi, the famed 11th century Biblical commentator, explains that God had not brought rain because He wanted the first human being to pray for it. Indeed, when Adam recognized the need for rain in the world, he prayed for it.

This is the first hint that the basic relationship between humanity and God is expressed through prayer. When Adam prays, he acknowledges that he has a relationship with God, he is dependent on God, and he must ask God for what he needs. As soon as Adam prays, God begins to relate to him directly and, of course, answers his prayer. Indeed, it rains and all the vegetation begins to sprout.

You see how it works?

We human beings don't really pray to have our needs met; we have needs in order that we pray. This is how we remind ourselves that God exists; this is how we build a relationship with Him.

The Bible teaches us that what happens to us is a direct consequence of our relationship with our Creator, because it is God Who is in charge of all that happens in the physical world.

Therefore, what happens to me—and how that which happens to me affects me—is determined by my relationship to this Master of the Universe. My relationship to this Master is monitored by my prayers, because that's how I interact with Him directly and immediately—it is how I speak to Him, it is how I hear Him, it is how I develop an emotional relationship with Him.

If I want certain developments to take place in this Universe, I appeal to Him. It's as simple as a hungry child appealing to his mother. "Mama, give me some cornflakes." The child knows he has a mother, he trusts her, he loves her, he depends on her. He knows that she is the center of his world. So, when he wants something, it's "Mama!" If he has hurt himself, it's "Mama!" If he needs help, it's "Mama!"

Of course, we need to remember that we are adults. We are not demanding, or whining, or throwing temper tantrums. We are addressing the Almighty, and we are seeking a mature relationship with Him.

And as any adult knows from life experience, for any relationship to stand a chance, it has to be real.

Being real with God means talking to Him from the heart.

Writes the 15th century philosopher Bachya Ben Joseph Ibn Paquda in his *Duties of the Heart*: "Understand that the words of prayer expressed by the mouth are merely the shell. The heart's meditation upon these words is the inner kernel. Words of prayer are like a body, while meditation is its soul. One who prays only with his tongue while his mind wanders resembles an empty body, a husk devoid of a kernel."

One can choose to pray through the recitation of blessings and psalms—in fact, the Sages advise it—but prayer can never be a "formality." It is not dashing off a bunch of words in a prescribed sequence. It is speaking to God—to our Creator, to our Father, to the Almighty—from the innermost recesses of our being.

The shortest prayer recorded in the Bible is the prayer of Moses when he discovered that his beloved sister, Miriam, has been afflicted with leprosy. He cries out to God from the depths of his being: "Please, Lord, heal her now."

His prayer is as searing as it is simple, and it captures his anguish and his complete faith in God that his prayer can and will be answered. And it is.

My friend Helen had such an experience when she learned that her son David had been diagnosed with a malignant tumor in his brain. The doctors advised that there wasn't much hope. But Helen refused to believe it. She said she began praying for a miracle with all her strength: "My intensity was of the highest degree there could be in this world. I sobbed my heart out not once but a hundred times a day. If I rolled over in bed, I prayed to God. If I sat up in bed, I prayed to God. I was praying every minute and I didn't stop praying." Not only that, she asked everyone she could think of to pray, too.

And it paid off—God answered her heartfelt prayer. David underwent successful surgery and radiation treatment. He is well on the way to recovery now, but Helen hasn't stopped praying.

Of course, the emotions we pour into our prayers when we plead for the recovery of a loved one from a serious illness cannot be readily mustered on an everyday basis. But we can go a long way to prepare ourselves, to create for ourselves an atmosphere of undisturbed concentration, to be aware of the words we speak and to whom we address them.

One of the most renowned of the Hassidic masters, Rav Nachman of Breslov, advocated finding a secluded place for prayer, preferably in nature, and there trying to address God from the heart, not worrying too much about the words at first: "As often as you can, take a trip out to the fields to pray. All the grasses will join you. They will enter your prayers and give you strength... when no words come, do not despair. Come back day after day to your secluded spot and wait. Just wanting to speak to God is in itself a very great thing. Even if all you can say to God is 'Help!' it is still good. Repeat this over and over again, until God opens your lips and words begin to flow from your heart."

Rav Nachman's message is as simple as it is powerful: Be real before God and He will meet you half-way.

King David promises us in Psalm 145: "The Almighty is near to all those who call unto Him in truth."

"In truth" means in sincerity.

One of the best examples of a sincere prayer I know—a prayer that was answered—comes from a fellow named Jeff, who at the time of his prayer was an avowed atheist.

Jeff, an MBA student from Harvard, had come to Jerusalem on his summer vacation, and, like every tourist, came to see the famous Western Wall of the Temple remains, better known the world over as the Wailing Wall.

As he relates the story, when he came to the Wall he thought that he was going to see some old stones and archeological digs. But he was amazed, because something more happened—he was suddenly overcome by a feeling he had never experienced before. He was shaken by a realization that he was standing on the site where once-upon-a-time, a certain people in ancient times had a special relationship with God and could communicate with Him freely. So Jeff, thinking he might tap into some of those vibrations, decided to pray.

Looking at the mammoth stones, he began, "God, I don't believe in You. As far as I know, You don't exist. But I do feel something, so maybe it's a possibility. Maybe I am making a mistake. If I am making a mistake, I want You to know, God, I'm not fighting You. I have no quarrel. It's just that I don't know You exist. But God, just in case You really are there and I'm making a mistake, do me a favor and get me an introduction."

Jeff's sincere attitude was palpable and another person took notice of him with his cardboard yarmulke on his head that gave him away as a novice. This person, seeing that Jeff was so clearly praying from the heart, on an impulse decided to approach him and invite him to a religious seminar in Bible studies.

So, as it happened, seconds after Jeff asked God for an introduction, he felt a hand tapping him on the shoulder.

Jeff jumped and whirled around to find a meek-looking fellow standing there. "What do you want?" he demanded.

The poor guy immediately apologized. "I'm so sorry, I just wanted to ask you if you wanted to learn about God."

Jeff turned white. It hit him like a 2-by-4 over the head. Now it was his turn to apologize. And, of course, he accepted the man's invitation and sat in on some Bible classes for about six weeks, and then he went back to Harvard a changed man. But, there is more to the story.

While he was in Jerusalem, he was sitting in a square one day when he noticed a very pretty, sweet-looking, modestly dressed young woman walking by. The fleeting thought he had could hardly be called a prayer by anyone's definition. It was a random thought, but it was addressed to God. He remembered thinking, "Please God, send me such a woman for a wife some day."

A year later, near Harvard, he saw the same young woman.

He couldn't help himself. "Excuse me, but I could swear that I saw you last summer in Jerusalem."

She smiled. "Yes, I was there. And I remember—I saw you, too."

Well, I don't have to tell you the rest. Suffice it to say, they are happily married and living in New Jersey.

Another story similar to Jeff's—of a man's first prayer to God and how it was answered—came to my attention after *Powerful Prayers* was published. At the end of the book I had included an invitation for anyone who had a special prayer story to share it with me. An incredible letter arrived in the mail from a man named Michael, who began with: "For about ten years I was a self-pronounced atheist. I was also an alcoholic and suffered nearly continuous severe depression. My only solace from an unhealthy mind was drink, and a sense of self-worth derived from unstable relationships with others, namely women."

He then went on to say that one day it all changed. The following excerpt from his long letter explains what happened: "My most recent girlfriend had left me and I was crushed. I hadn't slept in days and was drinking enormously. I had driven to my brother Tony's house to talk and cry and to tell him I had reached the end of my rope [and] that I had been wishing that something terrible would happen to me so that my suffering would end.

"That's when he told me about prayer and God. He said although I hadn't realized he was a believer, he was. He said it might seem weird to me, but that since I had nothing to lose, I was to go home, get on my knees, and ask God for help, even if I didn't believe.

"So I did. On my knees I told God I was scared and weak, that I didn't believe and that I wanted to die. I asked God to let me know He is there and to give me reason to go on. Then I waited. For the first time in my life I believed. For the rest of that day I watched and waited for God's answer.

"Sometime later in the evening, one my good friends, Nadine, called to tell me that she was standing at a pay phone, and that she was witnessing possibly the most beautiful rainbow she had ever seen. She called for no other reason than to tell me about it, because she knew I'd appreciate it.

"Out of the dark, there was a sudden glimmer of hope. In that one simple gift, God taught me as much as any man need ever know about Him; that He is there, that He loves me."

Michael knew that ever since the time of Noah's flood, the rainbow was God's special sign to humankind that He is there, still loving us no matter how much we disappoint Him.

Michael's and Jeff's stories illustrate that a key factor in prayer—wherever it is spoken or even thought—is sincerity. Even though both men were atheists, they were being real at the moment that they prayed. And on the spot, their prayers were answered.

"Prayers transform a stumbling block
into a steppingstone, a problem into
a pearl, a peril into a prize."

Moshe Goldberger,
*The Road to Greatness: How to Get Where You Want to Be*

By this time, you should have a clear idea in your mind who it is you are praying to—your Father in Heaven Who loves you and wants to give you anything you ask for.

You are now praying with the full expectation of getting your prayers answered and are aware that prayer is a relationship with God.

You recognize that prayer is an outpouring of the heart and that anything less is simply not good enough. You have chosen a place where you can address God with the attention He deserves and you want to reach Him sincerely and explain your needs and wants.

You are poised for the experience of having your prayers answered. And they will be. *All* prayers are answered. The catch is that sometimes the answer is *no.*

❧

# Step Two

Imagine that you are now driving through New York City and the rush hour has just begun. Traffic is slowing down.

Gridlock is imminent. You worry you will be stuck in your car well into the evening.

But why should you worry? There is no need. Your father owns everything in the city, including the company regulating all the traffic lights.

You call him on the car phone and ask for help.

Moments later, you are driving along and every light turns green on your approach. Zing ding, green light, green light, green light.

After a few blocks, it is happening so readily and so easily that you go on autopilot. The radio is playing some nice music. You are humming along, hardly paying attention to the world around you.

But then, suddenly, you hit a red light.

What?!

You snap to and slam on the brakes. You are shocked! Your father has the power to make all the lights green. He has done it for the past hour. So what went wrong at 42nd and Broadway?

This is the second step to getting your prayers answered—you have to be shocked when God doesn't grant your request. He has already given you so much, so why stop here?

Chances are that God wanted you to take pause and ponder this very question.

But most people react differently. Not having really believed that God can and will answer all their prayers, they are not even surprised. They just find their suspicions confirmed and stop moving forward.

Being shocked when things go wrong is an essential part of the process. It confirms that you really have prayed sincerely, believing in an all-powerful and all-loving God Who has your best interests at heart.

# Summary of
# Step Two:

# Be Shocked if You Don't
# Get What You Ask For

"God answers sharp and sudden on some prayers, and thrusts the thing we have prayed for in our face, a gauntlet with a gift in it."

Elizabeth Barrett Browning

To be real with God and prayer, you have to be shocked when things don't go smoothly for you. Your first reaction should be: "God is my Father in Heaven, why isn't He taking care of me?"

Of course, nothing God does is by accident. So now you have to ask: "Why is God doing this? Why is He trying to get my attention?"

And the most natural question that should follow must be: "Have I stopped paying attention?"

If you have stopped paying attention, then it is logical that God might want to get you back on track.

When you forget, or take for granted that God routinely moves mountains for you, things stop flowing and God tries to get you to refocus.

As was noted earlier, a relationship is a two-way street. A real relationship can't sustain itself if only one side cares.

# How to Pray a Better Way

❧

"Pray with emotion, and God will forgive you. Pray with an attentive heart, and see all of heaven's doors open before you. Pray with joy, and watch your requests ascend straight to God's chamber."

Rav Nachman of Breslov

A good friend of mine, Motty, suffered a minor stroke recently. While in the middle of a speech, he suddenly experienced total blindness in one eye. It didn't hurt and he finished what he had to say. Leisurely, he returned home, but since he still couldn't see out of the one eye, he decided it was best to call a doctor. The doctor told him to get himself to the hospital immediately. There Motty learned that he had experienced a stroke, and although his eyesight returned within hours, he was warned that he was not out of the woods yet. A stroke often has aftershocks, and all that medicine can do is watch and wait. Frightened by what was happening, Motty prayed as hard as he knew how, promising God all the while that he would be a better person. He was most fortunate that there were no further repercussions, and he went home totally unimpaired by what had happened.

Filled with gratitude to God for having healed him, he realized that, as a result of the bargains and promises he made, he was now on his way to becoming a much better human being. Then he realized that he had to be grateful to God for that, too. And then it hit him. God loved him so much, wanted him to be the best he could be so much, that He had sent him the frightening experience of a stroke to make sure he got on with his self-improvement program. And only then did he realize what he really needed to be grateful for—not so much for the healing, but for the stroke! Suddenly, gratitude took on a whole new meaning for him.

An attitude of gratitude—that is, being grateful for everything God sends us—is a key to praying effectively. And it is a quality that takes some effort to cultivate on a daily basis.

One of my teachers, Rabbi Zelig Pliskin, relates the story in his book, *Gateway to Happiness*, of a man who one day decided to spend a few minutes appreciating his morning cup of coffee. It was a part of his daily routine and, God forbid, if something went wrong and he had to go without it, he sure missed it. As he began to ponder this cup of coffee, he jotted down his thoughts. First of all he noted that coffee beans grew in Brazil, and someone had to plant the trees and tend them until the coffee beans reached maturity. Workers had to pick the beans from the trees and then the beans had to be roasted, and ground and packed for shipping. There was tremendous work involved in the shipping industry, which allowed the coffee to reach the United States—this alone required hundreds of people. Finally, the coffee beans arrived in his grocery store. But that was not all. The water for the coffee was boiled on a gas range and the story of the manufacture and delivery of that appliance into his kitchen could easily fill a book. Then there was the gas, the water, and the kettle that whistled to let him know the water had boiled. The match couldn't be left out. He drank his coffee with milk, so the dairy industry had to be considered and all the work involved from the time the milk left the cow until it reached his coffee cup. At the end of writing furiously for a half-hour, the man had not even begun to describe the cup, saucer and teaspoon he used, the table he placed them on, or the chair he sat in. For the first time, he became aware of the thousands of people whose work was necessary for him to have that cup of coffee. This awareness led him to a most intense spiritual experience. His prayers for the next few weeks were permeated with a deep feeling of gratitude to his fellow human beings, all of whom made it possible for him to exist on this planet.

Now, that's what appreciating a cup of coffee did for this man. But what about all the things that had happened that same morning *before* he even came into the kitchen? These same things happen to all of us in much the same order, and we can easily imagine the sequence of events: First, he woke up—there, he was alive! He opened his eyes and watched the objects in his bedroom come into focus. Yes, he had eyesight. Then he moved his hand to rub his eyes. For his hand to move, thousands of electrical and chemical changes had to take place in his body and travel from his brain to his arm. He looked at the alarm clock, "Oh boy, I better get going." He didn't give it a second thought that everything in his body was functioning just fine—he had eyesight, he had mobility, he had consciousness. Although God made sure that he had all these things, he took them for granted each and every day much the same way he had taken his coffee for granted.

When his coffee wasn't there one morning, he missed it. He appreciated it more when he was deprived of it, when he had run out of coffee beans, or the oven malfunctioned and he couldn't boil water. How much more would he have missed his eyesight, his limbs, his mind!

Just think where you'd be without those seemingly simple gifts. According to government statistics, 50,000 Americans are blinded each year—that means *one every minute*! So eyesight is nothing to be taken for granted, as my friend Motty learned from his short experience with temporary blindness.

The saying goes: "There for the grace of God, go I." Indeed that is so true. God is looking out for us every second of the day. Yet, we just assume when things are going well, that this is how it should be. But we can't take anything for granted, as just a cursory look around should tell us. Therefore, by reminding ourselves that eyesight, mobility, consciousness and freedom come from God, we awaken our appreciation for His love and care, which are as infinite as God is Himself.

This is why the Sages advise that, before we start beseeching God with a long litany of our requests, we should acknowledge all that He has done for us already.

My prayer book, drawing on a tradition two-thousand years old, lists blessings to be said each morning over life's essentials: "Blessed are You Lord, Our God, Ruler of the Universe... Who gives sight to the blind... Who releases the imprisoned... Who straightens the bent... Who guides the steps of man... Who gives strength to the weary... Who provided me with all my needs...

Beginning each day with such a reminder might go a long way toward not taking God for granted. When we appreciate what we've already been given, God will want to give us more.

There is a story told about an uncle who was financing his nephew's college education. Naturally, the uncle was anxious to know how the nephew was coming along, but no matter how many times he asked, the nephew would never write. He was always too busy; and to be absolutely frank, he was taking his uncle's generosity for granted.

So, one day, the uncle wrote the nephew a note, asking once again about his progress. And, although he added, "I am enclosing the usual check to cover your expenses," to the note, he intentionally left the check out. Within days, as the uncle had hoped, there arrived a nice letter from the nephew about his classes and grades, and at the end, the nephew had added: "By the way, you forgot to enclose the check."

God does the same thing. He not only gives us life, but supports and sustains us at every moment. He wants to hear from time to time how we are doing—He wants a personal report. If too much time goes by without a connection, God sends us the equivalent of a letter with a missing check just to refocus our attention—to remind us of the source of our well being.

The Sages teach us that while every day we should begin with the attitude of appreciation, our prayers should go beyond just that. Ideal prayer includes three components: **praise**, **requests**, and **thanks**.

Now, some people might think that these three ingredients for prayer are a bit puzzling. Nobody has much trouble with the requests part, but praising God often hangs people up: "What does God need praise for? Does He have a weak ego or something?"

It's true that at first glance praise may seem a strange way to start. It may feel like trying to butter up God. But it would be absurd to suggest that by reciting a prayer of praise we can actually succeed in flattering God. Objectively speaking, it would require infinite praise to properly praise an infinite being. From God's perspective, anything less would be clearly inadequate.

Clearly, God doesn't need it. But we do.

We need to spell out for ourselves who God is. Praising God helps us to realize how all-encompassing God's reality is and tune into that reality. It also helps us become more sensitive to God's awesome capacity to answer our prayers.

That brings us to our specific requests—the segment of prayer that a friend of mine calls "the please, please me" part.

Nobody needs to be told what to pray for—most people have a wish-list a mile long. But we must keep in mind that as an ideal parent, God always gives us exactly what we need. Therefore, as noted earlier, whatever happens to us in our lives is actually a direct function of who we are. If we were different, God would be giving us different things.

So, when we pray for something that hasn't yet been given to us, what we are really trying to do is change ourselves into the kind of person who would merit receiving what we are asking for!

That is why the Hebrew term for prayer is *li-heet-pallel.* The word *pallel* means to "inspect." The prefix *li-heet* makes the verb reflexive, that is, a verb that reflects back onto the subject. Therefore, praying becomes an act of introspection. When we pray we take an honest look inside and ask with humility:

"What do I need to change about myself in order to get what I really want out of life?"

There is a legend that if you pray at the Wailing Wall in Jerusalem for whatever you want over 40 consecutive days, without skipping a single day, your prayer will be answered.

A friend of mine, a fellow named Shraga, decided to test this out. At that time, he had been thinking about getting married and so he was going to be praying for a wife. He had a very definite idea of what kind of woman he wanted to marry, and he decided to pray for 40 days for that specific person to cross his path, look his way and say "I do." A tall order, but as God runs the Universe, Shraga thought, this should be a snap for him.

As Shraga tells it, "At first I treated this exercise of praying for 40 days straight as some kind of magical metaphysical ploy to butter up God and score brownie points. But as the days passed, I began to understand the power of prayer. Because it occurred to me to ask: 'What would a woman with the qualities I desired want in a husband? Would she not have very high standards also? Would I meet these standards?' As I prayed I realized that I had to work on myself to be worthy. I went through a period of self-examination and solidified my commitment to confront my shortcomings and developed a plan to overcome them."

The remarkable thing is that two days after his 40 days of praying were up, Shraga met his wife Keren, and she was everything he had prayed for. God had answered his prayer. But Shraga was not the same man who started praying some six weeks before.

Shraga had discovered the power of prayer as a tool of self-transformation, besides developing the habit of connecting with God every day.

As you connect with God through prayer, you will be changed. There is no doubt about it. The sincerity and honesty of prayer—though you may direct it to heaven—will also shine a powerful light on yourself.

In so doing, you will discover why it is that God said no to a particular request. Were you perhaps asking for the wrong thing without realizing it at first?

An ideal parent will not lend the car keys to a teenager who is not yet responsible enough to handle driving it. Similarly, you might not be ready to receive what you are praying for until you do some work to earn it.

Self-transformation means that tomorrow you may not be the same person to whom God said no yesterday. Self-transformation means that you can make of yourself a person who deserves a yes.

When making your requests, you might want to keep in mind this tip from the Talmud: it is best to ask for others needs first. Why? Because if you are able to put your problems aside and see what others are lacking, you are showing God that you attained a level of sensitivity which merits your prayers being answered.

My prayer book contains a list of "suggested" requests—known as *Shmoney Esrey* or the "Eighteen Benedictions." Included in that list are prayers for healing, for peace, for wisdom. I found, as I discovered the power of prayer as a tool of self-examination, that praying for success and wealth somehow pales next to a prayer for world peace.

Finally, in the concluding thanks section, it is important to take inventory of all that you have been given and acknowledge how you've come by it all. (Hint: not by your own brains or brawn.)

This is a very useful reminder. God doesn't need your thanks any more than He needs your praise, but you need to thank God for your own sake, so you don't begin to fool yourself into thinking that you—and not God—brought about all the good things in your life.

Just think for a moment: If you were God, would you keep extending yourself even further for someone who has barely noticed what you have already given him or her? Or who takes credit for your blessings?

Am I right? Case closed.

Composer and singer Sam Glazer wrote a beautiful song incorporating the words of the morning prayer *Thankful, I Am*. Sam's rendition captures the simple essence of this prayer:

---

Good morning to the world, thank you for this day,
Thank you for the gift of life You always send my way...

What am I going to sing, what am I going to do,
To show how much I feel for you?

Thank you for the sun, thank you for the moon,
Thank you for the words that fit so nicely in this tune

Before I wash my face, before I brush my hair,
I recognize You're everywhere.

from *A Day in the Life* by Sam Glazer

Okay, hopefully you have been duly shocked out of your complacency—that is, if you were guilty of it.

You have discovered that God says no to some prayers in order to help you refocus.

Why?

Well, perhaps you weren't appreciative of what you've been given. Perhaps you were taking God and all His incredible gifts for granted. Perhaps you needed to be sensitized to God's awesome capacity to help you. Perhaps you were looking for the easy way out and weren't investing in your own growth. Perhaps you just weren't ready.

But now you have done some sincere soul searching. You have discovered the power of prayer as a tool of self-examination. You are working hard on who it is you want to become. You are praying in a totally new way, reminding yourself who God is and what He has done for not only you, but for all of us.

❦

# Step Three

I magine that you are on a winding mountain road, and you are driving cautiously, because there is a steep cliff off to your right.

As you make your way around one particularly treacherous curve, suddenly you come face to face with a huge truck barreling toward you at full speed.

In a flash you realize that, in another instant, the truck is going to crash into you head on. To avoid certain death, you swerve to the right and find yourself in a free fall down the steep cliff.

"Dear God, please save me!" you call out, terrified.

It all takes mere seconds, but it feels like hours as you hold your breath to see where you will land and if you will come out alive.

Incredibly, miraculously, the car falls into a thick outgrowth of bushes, and, other than being shaken by the experience, you are perfectly fine.

Naturally, you are filled with gratitude. Your life was spared. "Thank You God. Thank You God. Thank You God," you mutter under your breath.

Now consider: Who do you think pushed you off the cliff in the first place? The answer is as obvious as it is alarming, and therein lies the reason for God's actions.

God wants us to ask "Why did you do this to me?" in order to get our attention!

When that happens, it's important not to get angry or resentful, but to take the message to heart and learn from it.

God is always teaching us. God is not arbitrary or unfair. God is not punishing us; He is educating us to make us better. Becoming bitter signifies that we have forgotten that God is our loving parent; it only indicates to God that we still have much to learn. If we refuse to hear and continue to be resentful of the lessons He is trying to teach us, then the distance between us and God is likely to grow wider.

Prayer is a relationship with God and as such it is not a one-way street. God responds to our needs and teaches us lessons that we had no idea we needed to learn. Hearing God is just as important as talking to God and is an essential part of what prayer is all about.

# Summary of Step Three:

# Pay Attention to What God is Teaching You

"And behold, the Lord passed by.
There was a great and mighty wind,
splitting mountains and shattering
rocks by the power of the Lord; but the
Lord was not in the wind.
After the wind—an earthquake;
but the Lord was not in the earthquake.
After the earthquake—fire; but the
Lord was not in the fire.
And after the fire—a soft murmuring voice."

I Kings 19:11-12

By now, you probably can see how these various components of prayer are all parts of one piece. It's all about recognizing God, transforming yourself so you can have a relationship with God, talking to God, and... yes... hearing God.

When you open your heart to God in prayer, you will find that the communication is no longer one way—you will have tuned into a frequency where you can hear God as well as speak to Him.

But you have to tune into God, just as you would tune into a radio. To hear the music that is being broadcast on the radio, you need to tune in to the right station. The same applies with God.

God is always broadcasting, but precious few tune in. To tune in on the correct frequency you have to make of yourself a well-functioning receiver. And only then can you get God's message.

# How to Decode God's Message

❧

"Two prisoners whose cells adjoin communicate with each other by knocking on the wall. The wall is the thing which separates them but is also their means of communication. It is the same with us and God. Every separation is a link."

Simone Weil, *Gravity and Grace*

A student of mine named Ronnie was found to have a tumor behind her eye, which had to be removed surgically. Although the tumor was benign, the needed operation was to be quite complicated due to the tumor's proximity to the brain, requiring two surgeons—an eye specialist and a neurologist—working together. In addition to the risk of brain damage, permanent blindness was also a possibility.

Ronnie was terrified by what awaited her and found herself emotionally paralyzed and unable to pray. Seeing her terror, a close friend brought her the book, My Father, My King, written by Rabbi Zelig Pliskin. Using the Bible as his guide, Rabbi Pliskin wrote the book in the form of a hundred short messages from God, each one answering a different situational dilemma.

Ronnie opened the book quite randomly and found herself reading: "When you experience fear, hear your Father, your King, the Creator and Sustainer of the entire Universe, saying to you: 'My child, let Me help you over your fears... I am always with you...'"

It was precisely what Ronnie needed to hear. She started to cry as the gentle words of love and reassurance swept over her. The remarkable thing is that when she flipped the page again, her eyes fell on the following story:

"Rabbi Lederberg who lived in Jerusalem, ran a business to earn a living and spent all the time that remained studying the Bible. Once he became sick and needed surgery to his head. The doctors told him that after the operation, which was needed to save his life, he might never see again..."

Ronnie gasped. This is what was happening to her.

The story went on to relate how the rabbi memorized large chunks of Biblical commentaries so he would never forget them if he lost his sight and was unable to read. Fortunately, the surgery was a success and not only did it save the rabbi's life, but it saved his vision.

The same happened with Ronnie—her operation was also a success. What she'd read had given her the strength she needed to face her operation and the lengthy recuperation after. She really felt God was with her, sending her His love in the messages from the book. Today, she reports using Rabbi Pliskin's book quite often, flipping to a random page and finding there a message from God that fits the moment perfectly.

We all want a connection with God when we are troubled and having a hard time finding answers to difficult questions. The Sages advise us that the best way to hear God is by reading and studying the Bible.

In the Book of Exodus, the Bible tells us that God spoke to the Israelite nation at Mount Sinai and in a simple, clear way spelled out how we human beings could forge a relationship with Him and how we could have our prayers answered.

God's voice from Sinai has never ceased. It resonates today and the easiest way to tune into it is by studying God's word in the Bible. It will teach you what this relationship between you and God is all about and why it is so important to your life.

For one thing, you will learn from studying the Bible that there is a symbiotic relationship between what you do and what God does. There seem to be strings attached between us and God.

In the Middle Ages there were philosophers who, realizing this truth, questioned the presence of free will in man. They wondered if God wields all the power and we are just puppets on strings.

But the 11th century genius Maimonides argued that there absolutely is free will, but that humanity clearly has a purpose and a mission on earth as well—we do have a mandate from God. That mandate says, "Go, do as you will, but make the world a better place."

The Kabbalists take this a step further. They say that there really are strings between us and God. When things happen in the world, we see the strings and we see God's hand. But here is the beauty of it: It's not God Who is pulling the strings, it's us—we are pulling the strings.

How can this be?

Well, God has given us the rules by which He operates—the spiritual rules of the Universe. When we act in accordance with the rules, there is rain, crops grow, we eat and are satisfied, we prosper and life is good. So, when we follow the rules, we are pulling the strings, because when we do so, God must act. God always acts in accordance with the rules that He Himself has given us.

Moses summarized the rules for us in this succinct passage from his farewell address to the Israelites, found in the Book of Deuteronomy [11:13-17]: *"If, then, you obey the commandments that I enjoin upon you this day—to love the Lord your God and to serve Him with all your heart and soul—God will grant the rain for your land in season, the early rain and the late rain. You shall gather in your grain and wine and oil. God will provide grass in the fields for your cattle. And you will eat and be satisfied. But take care not to be lured away to serve other gods and bow to them. For the Lord's anger will blaze against you and He will restrain the skies so that there will be no rain and the ground will not yield its produce, and you will soon perish..."*

You have enormous power in your hands. Everything you do matters. This reality gives an incredible importance to humanity. And that is an awesome thing to realize.

When you act in a good way, God will respond that way. When you act in a bad way, God will respond accordingly. The decision is totally yours. Those are the rules of the spiritual Universe and they are clearly spelled out in the Bible. And if you should know only one thing, it should be that God plays by the rules.

Once you understand that the condition of the world is dependent upon each and every one of us, and that to do the job you must have a relationship with God, then prayer—as a key factor in that relationship—becomes an essential ingredient in your life. To this end, a relationship with God is essential, communicating with God is essential, transforming yourself so that you fulfill your mission is essential.

The person who seemed to have been the first to realize all that and who put it together for us as a model to follow is Abraham, the father of ethical monotheism.

One of the most poignant stories of the Bible tells us what kind of person Abraham was, at the same time illustrating graphically what we are doing here on earth.

As the story opens, Abraham, who just a day earlier made his covenant with God, is praying. The Bible relates: *"God appeared to him in the plains of Mamrei, as he was sitting at the opening of his tent in the heat of the day. He lifted his eyes and saw and there were three men coming up toward him. He saw them and ran from the tent to greet them..."*

Incredible. God had appeared to Abraham and they were having a personal conversation. As hard as we might pray to get close to God, it's highly unlikely we will ever get that close. Yet, Abraham *interrupted* his prayer to greet some strangers. He said, "Sorry God, there's somebody at the door. See you later." Why?

In this very clear message the Bible is telling us that acting with kindness toward others—acting *like* God—is more important than talking *to* God. It is more important to help others than to enjoy a spiritual high alone.

We are in this world to make it a better place, to fix it, to unite with others in brotherhood, peace and harmony, in short to live up to the promise of our creation when God formed the human being "after His likeness." And we pray to learn from God how to do that. And God always answers loud and clear on that one.

A friend of mine named Uriela decided to take a trip into the Sinai Peninsula, secretly hoping for a spiritual experience. This was the place, she knew, where the Israelites had their profound encounter with God, which changed them—and indeed, the world—forever. Some of those spiritual vibrations were bound to be hanging around; she wanted to see if she could tune in.

The goal of the trip was to reach the highest spot in the Sinai open to tourists—Mount Abbas Basha—and see the sunset from there. It took three hours by Bedouin cab, three hours by camel and another two hours walking. She found herself in stunning territory, surrounded by mammoth, wind-shorn rocks reaching like tall arms to the sky. Here was land where nothing grew, not even a blade of grass, and no birds or any other sign of life interrupted the forbidding vistas. It was awesome.

But, as Uriela and her guide rested prior to taking on the last climb just before sunset, the stillness was broken by voices and three hikers appeared from nowhere. Uriela was very surprised to see other people amid such isolation, but she became annoyed when the hikers decided to take a rest next to her little encampment. "Can't they find another place to sit?" she muttered to her guide. "They've got the whole Sinai. Why do they choose to impinge on my space?"

And then it hit her. It wasn't her space; it was God's space. And how different was her attitude toward these three strangers than Abraham's had been toward his three visitors. She did an immediate 180-degree spin and offered the hikers some of her food.

"No thank you," they said, and promptly left.

Uriela is convinced today that they were sent there for this very purpose. She had prayed for a spiritual experience and her prayers were answered—although not in the way she had imagined.

That trip to the Sinai proved to be a redefining experience for Uriela. Henceforth, she made it a point of being hospitable and would frequently have large groups to dinner, among whom many "strangers" were present. And it led to other, significant changes in her life. She always thought of herself as a good person, but the process of self-examination that began in the Sinai led her to realize that she was not a "good" person—she was merely "not bad." She never hurt people and was generally nice. But putting herself out for strangers —doing something actively good—was not part of her life plan. All this changed for her dramatically, and she says she never ceases to be grateful to God for that.

The important factor in Uriela's story is that she would never have heard the message if she had not been familiar with the Abraham story. The message would have come—the strangers would have arrived, sat down, annoyed her—but she wouldn't have known what to make of it. It would have been rather like a radio broadcast in a foreign language, with idiomatic references she could not decode.

And this is why, of course, the Sages advise that to hear God one must study the Bible. Then when you do tune in to God's message, you can understand it. You will grasp the big picture and how all the little pieces fit together to make of you the best that you can be.

I asked for strength, and
God gave me difficulties to make me strong.
I asked for wisdom, and
God gave me problems to solve.
I asked for prosperity, and
God gave me brawn and brain to work.
I asked for courage, and
God gave me dangers to overcome.
I asked for love, and
God gave me troubled people to help.
I asked for favors, and
God gave me opportunities.
I received nothing I wanted.
I received everything I needed.
My prayers were answered.

—Anonymous

God is always teaching us—and sometimes the lessons are gentle, sometimes more forceful, sometimes painful.

Certain people like to talk about God as if He were some kind of "Superman," Who is off in a faraway land, but Who will fly to our rescue when we call out to Him in distress. God is not far away; God is involved in our lives at every moment. Indeed, He often brings about tests in our lives in order to help us grow spiritually, and He can always be counted on to help us meet those challenges and become better people as a result of the experiences we encounter.

Often we know very well what parts of our selves need work but we become so preoccupied with the physical aspects of living that we neglect the spiritual.

C.S. Lewis wrote: "Pain is God's megaphone to wake up a deaf world." But we don't need to let it go that far. Prayer shows us a way of living—relating to God, working on one's self, changing for the better—so that we don't need to have such rude awakenings. But if we do wind up there, prayer also shows us the way out.

When disaster strikes we are all too ready to make self-improvements in order to bargain with God. We find strength to change ourselves if we really want something from God. If that is true of you, are you not tempting God?

Think about it: If God wants to bring out the best in you, if God wants you to have a relationship with Him, and if God knows that the only way you will stretch yourself that far is when something bad happens, then are you not asking for it?

Is it not better to start now on your own, rather than waiting until things go wrong and you are prodded into doing what you really wanted to do anyway, but which you put off and put off until God sends you a strong message: "Get going already!" So, get going now!

# ❧

# Step Four

Whenever you don't get what you want from God, you have to assume that it would not have been good for you. You have to assume that God knows much better than you do just what is good for you right now.

So the fourth step in getting your prayers answered is: Re-examine your request if you don't get what you asked for.

Were you asking for an easy life? For wealth? For tools to become a better person? Why were you making that specific request?

You have to know why you want something in order to judge if it would be good for you or not. If you are trying to become a better person, God is not going to give you something that will work against that. Instead, God will hear your prayer and present you with challenges that will help you in this objective.

Prayer helps you refine and affirm what it is you want out of life. If God gave you everything without you asking for it, you'd be spoiled. You would never be forced to really choose what you want in life. You'd get everything on a silver platter, but you'd never grow.

Ultimately, prayer is not about telling God what you need. God already knows—and much better than we ever could—what that is. Ultimately, prayer is about defining your choices in life and stating these choices out loud so both you and God can hear.

# Summary of Step Four:

# Re-evaluate Your Request

"When you pray, think. Think well what you're saying and make your thoughts into things that are solid.
In that way, your prayer will have strength, and that strength will become a part of your body, mind and spirit."

Walter Pidgeon to Roddy McDowall in
*How Green Was My Valley*

If an airplane, leaving Los Angeles for New York, is just a quarter degree off course, it will—because such is the law of physics and geometry—end up in northern Canada. If you don't believe me, position a ruler on a map and see what happens when the line is straight between point A (Los Angeles) and B (New York), and when it is just a smidgen off at point A. You will see that it then cannot connect with point B.

The importance of the choices you make today cannot be underestimated. What you choose now will have far reaching repercussions for the rest of your life.

Yes, you will always have the opportunity to pray and change the course of your life, but if your choices led you to Nova Scotia, it may take a lot of praying and hard work to get up the fare for New York. And think of the time and the energy you would have wasted.

Historian A.J. Toynbee, analyzing the "what if's" of history for the *New York Times* [March 5, 1961] concluded that: "We human beings do have some genuine freedom of choice and therefore some effective control over our own destinies... but the decisive choice is seldom the latest choice in the series. More often than not, it will turn out to be some choice made relatively far back in the past."

So get in touch with your deepest spiritual desires. Decide now what it is that you truly want out of life. Tell it to yourself and tell it to God. Then go for it. For sure, God will help. You can count on it.

# How to Choose
# What You Really Want

❦

"One of the annoying things about believing
in free choice and individual responsibility
is the difficulty of finding somebody to blame
your problems on. And when you do find
somebody, it's remarkable how often his
picture turns up on your driver's license."

P.J. O'Rourke, in *Rolling Stone* magazine

❧

My teacher, Rabbi Noah Weinberg, is fond of telling a story of how one day, when he was a kid, he decided to play hooky from school and, along with some of his classmates, go see the World's Fair in New York. Unfortunately, the admission fee was a dollar, which he didn't have. But all the other kids were going and he wanted very much to go, too.

Then it hit him. Maybe if he walked around he'd find a dollar on the street. People lost money from time to time. He'd found coins on the ground before. With eyes glued to the pavement, he started his search.

As he was looking he thought it might be a good idea to increase his chances by praying. "Almighty, please help me out here. Let me find a dollar just this one time. Just one dollar. It's nothing to You, right?"

Then he threw in some bargaining chips for good measure, "You know Almighty, if You help me find a dollar, I'll take out the garbage and I won't fight with my sister."

But no dollar.

"Almighty, I'll do my homework every day."

Still no dollar.

"Almighty, if you let me find a dollar, just this once, I won't do anything wrong for the rest of my life!"

As soon as he said the words, it hit him. Who was he kidding? As soon as he found the dollar he was going to do something wrong—play hooky from school and have a good time at the World's Fair. He was asking for the dollar just so he could do something wrong!

The moral of the story is: Whatever you pray for, be sure that you are not fooling yourself and/or trying to fool God. Is what you want truly good for you?

Of course, the introspective aspects of prayer will go a long way to keep you on track. If your prayer is sincere, it will help you confront yourself honestly and come to terms with what it is you are asking for and why. Is it what you really want out of life?

For sure, even if you can fool yourself at times, you can't fool God. He knows exactly what you need. He can give you everything now, but He also knows that some things will be more precious to you after you earn them yourself and that you will be better for it.

We have said that "Our Father in Heaven" is richer than the richest billionaire, more powerful than all the presidents and leaders of all the superpowers on earth. He can do anything. So another reasonable question to ask is why do we experience any problems at all? Why doesn't God intervene in our difficulties and fix things that go wrong?

As any good parent knows, the worst thing you can do for your children is to do everything for them. By so doing you rob them of a sense of their own accomplishment, you rob them of their self-esteem. You can't live their lives for them. You can't control them at every turn. If you could live their lives for them, they would never become their own individual selves; should you accomplish such a feat, they'd just be clones of you. If you love your kids, you will allow them to move off on their own, to be independent.

Being independent is what makes life meaningful. We all want to have the pleasures and accomplishments of making our own choices. If we were just robots, mechanically following every instruction, the world might be neat and tidy, but life wouldn't be life.

If God wanted to create us as robots, He would have. But He didn't. God wants us to make our own choices. He gave human beings the power to make decisions that are eternally meaningful.

But if our choices are to have real significance, they must be of our own free will. That is why, with all His power, God won't live our lives for us. He gives us our space. If we choose to move away from God, He will let us do that.

Just as He allowed Adam and Eve to choose against Him, to choose against Paradise and for the Knowledge of Good and Evil (which means the experience of pain and suffering and death), God will also allow us the free choice to make our mistakes and turn away from the good He wants to give us. He will let us make the wrong choice, not because He wants to punish us, but because He wants us to have independence, even at the risk of it being misused. We may suffer the consequences, but that's our choice. We get to keep our independence—our free will—intact.

If God were to step in and prevent it whenever we were about to make a mistake, we would be severely limited in our choices. In fact, it would be impossible for us to choose freely. Without the ability to choose, we'd be denied the pleasure of a meaningful existence.

But God does not play games. In the Bible, He gives us the rules of the spiritual Universe clearly spelled out. Living life according to those rules means aligning ourselves with the will of God. It means developing a close relationship with Him. It means figuring out what our mission is here on earth and finding out how to accomplish it in the most efficient manner possible.

The clearest summary of God's hopes and wishes for us can be found in the

Book of Deuteronomy, where Moses admonishes the Israelites to align their lives with the will of the Almighty. He concludes by telling them: *"I call heaven and earth to witness against me this day. I have put before you life and death, blessing and curse—choose life!"* [Deuteronomy 30:19]

Don't make the mistake of Adam and Eve. They chose the Tree of Knowledge of Good and Evil, which brought them death, when they could have chosen to eat from the other tree in the Garden of Eden—the Tree of Life.

But it's not too late. Each one of us gets to choose all over again.

We can all choose life and find all our prayers answered. We can find our way back to where we belong, back to the Garden of Eden, in the blissful embrace of a loving God, our Father in Heaven.

"God himself has told us that God wishes things which do not happen because man does not wish them! Thus the rights of man are immense, and his greatest misfortune is to be unaware of them."

Joseph de Maistre

This is it.

You are clear on Who God is. You know what prayer is and how to go about it.

You know why you are praying and what you're praying for.

You have come to terms with what you want from God. You are honest with yourself and know what you have to do to become the person to whom God says yes.

You have learned how to pay attention to God. You are tuning into God's voice.

You are working hard to be the best you can be and to fulfill your mission on earth. You have chosen life and all the best it has to offer.

### ✌

# Step Five

The story is told that when the Israelites were escaping from slavery in Egypt and the Pharaoh's army was pursuing them, they came to a dead end—the Red Sea. Of course, they panicked and cried out to heaven in prayer. But nothing happened. They wept and prayed, but then one person, a man named Nahson, stepped into the water and started wading in deeper. He kept forging forward until the water was up to his nose. And then the miracle happened—the waves receded and the sea split.

Nahson taught us that you can't just stand on the shore praying, you have to jump in, and then God will aid your effort.

The bottom line is that you will get your prayers answered if you are clear about what you want, if you pray as if you expect to get it, if you are willing to honestly examine yourself at times when the answer is no, and if—and this is the big if—you are willing to put in the effort.

Your choice is not real until you are ready to get behind it. You have to choose and make a commitment to stand by your choice, act on your choice, and make your choice a reality.

Talk is cheap. Prayer is not an escape or a way to evade responsibility. If you are not willing to work for what you say you want, then that's an indication that you must not really want it.

If you are serious about what it is you are praying for, then you are going to do whatever you can to make it happen. And God will lend a hand. And then, and only then, you can expect to be pleasantly surprised. You can expect to get your prayers answered, because at last you will be in tune with what is best for you, with what God wants for you.

# Summary of Step Five:

# Put in the Effort

"Until one is committed there is hesitancy, the chance to draw back; always ineffectiveness. Concerning all acts of initiative (and creation) there is one elementary truth, the ignorance of which kills countless ideas and splendid plans: That the moment one definitely commits oneself, then Providence moves too. All sorts of things occur to help one that would never have occurred. A whole stream of events issue from the decision, raising in one's favor all manner of unforeseen incidents, and meetings and material assistance, which no man could have dreamt would have come his way. I have learned a deep respect for one of Goethe's couplets:
'Whatever you can do, whatever you can dream, begin it; boldness has genius, power and magic in it.'"

W.H. Murray, quoted in
*The Last Place on Earth* by Harold T.P. Hayes

There is a wonderful Native American folktale about a tribe that had been experiencing a prolonged drought and had decided to send for the rainmaker to change their misfortune.

After some days the rainmaker arrived with much fanfare and the tribespeople eagerly waited for him to do his thing, whatever it is that rainmakers do—dance the raindance, blow smoke signals to the sky to start the clouds rolling, call upon the Great Spirit in prayer...

But the rainmaker did none of those things.

Instead, he took a long time locating the perfect spot for his tee-pee and setting it up. Then he found the perfect river rocks to build his hearth and collected the necessary wood for the fire.

Meanwhile, the tribe was becoming impatient, and understandably so. They had been plagued by the drought for several months and had grown desperate. Finally, just when they couldn't stand it anymore—after three days of setting up his household—the rainmaker sat in front of his tee-pee cross-legged. He lifted his eyes to the sky and just then a thunderclap was heard. Moments later the rain came.

The point of the story is: "SET YOUR HOUSE IN ORDER AND IT WILL RAIN." Make yourself ready to receive God's blessing and it will come pouring down.

"The moment of absolute certainty never arrives. Above all, remember that God helps those who help themselves. Act as if everything depended upon you, and pray as if everything depended upon God."

S.H. Puyer

∽6

# In Conclusion

One of my all time favorite stories illustrating the awesome power of making the effort and having unbounded faith and hope that God answers prayers—in short, all the things we have been talking about in this book—comes from the Holocaust.

It happened in the Ukraine, at the Janowska Road Camp where the Jewish prisoners were rounded up one morning and brought before two huge pits, which, they soon realized, were going to be their common grave.

However, the Nazi guards decided to have some fun with the terrified victims, and so they ordered them to jump across the pits. Whoever managed to land on the other side would live; whoever didn't make it would be shot.

This is how Yaffa Eliach tells the story in *Hasidic Tales of the Holocaust* [New York: Vintage, 1988, pp.3-4]: "Among the thousand of Jews on that field in Janowska was the Rabbi of Bluzhov, Rabbi Israel Spira. He was standing with a friend, a freethinker from a large Polish town, whom the rabbi had met in the camp. A deep friendship had developed between the two.

"'Spira, all of our efforts to jump over the pits are in vain. We only entertain the Germans and their collaborators, the Askaris. Let's sit down in the pits and wait for the bullets to end our wretched existence,' said the friend to the rabbi.

"'My friend,' said the rabbi, as they were walking in the direction of the pits, 'man must obey the will of God. If it was decreed from heaven that pits be dug and we be commanded to jump, pits will be dug and jump we must. And if, God forbid, we fail and fall into the pits, we will reach the World of Truth a second later after our attempt. So, my friend, we must jump.'

"The rabbi and his friend were nearing the edge of the pits; the pits were rapidly filling up with bodies.

"The rabbi glanced down at his feet, the swollen feet of a fifty-three-year-old Jew ridden with starvation and disease. He looked at his young friend, a skeleton with burning eyes.

"As they reached the pit, the rabbi closed his eyes and commanded in a powerful whisper, 'We are jumping!' When they opened their eyes, they found themselves standing on the other side of the pit.

"'Spira, we are here, we are here, we are alive!' the friend repeated over and over again, while warm tears streamed from his eyes. 'Spira, for your sake, I am alive; indeed, there must be a God in heaven. Tell me, rabbi, how did you do it?'

"'I was holding on to my ancestral merit. I was holding on to the coattails of my father, and my grandfather, and my great-grandfather, of blessed memory,' said the rabbi and his eyes searched the black skies above. 'Tell me, my friend, how did you reach the other side of the pit?'

"'I was holding on to you,' replied the rabbi's friend."

Indeed, however the chain of faith was formed, ultimately they were all holding on to their Father in Heaven for Whom no request is too large or too small, too urgent or too outrageous.

Dare to ask for miracles and you will see them with your own eyes.

With hope and faith, may all your prayers be answered, and may you live each day as the miracle that it is.

# The Five Steps to Having Your Prayers Answered

✍

1. Pray like you expect results.

2. Be shocked if you don't get what you ask for.

3. Pay attention to what God is teaching you.

4. Re-evaluate your request.

5. Put in the effort.

❦

# Helpful Tips
# and Exercises

**1** If you have a hard time believing that your prayers have been answered, you need only remind yourself how often they have been in the past. God answered your prayers when you weren't even praying! How is that? Take out a piece of paper and list 100 blessings God has granted you in your lifetime. Next, from the list of 100, identify your top 10. You can readily see now how much God loves you and how much He has given you already. Now call a friend and share your list.

❦

2   To find the place of sincerity within yourself from which you can address God, it can be helpful to go out among nature. Sites of awesome beauty—oceans, mountains, canyons—often inspire us to pour our hearts to God. Go to such a spot, away from other people, and let yourself feel your soul's inner yearning. Articulate what it is you sincerely desire. Ask God to fulfill it.

❧

3   Identify a place in or near your home that you can visit daily for a few quiet moments of seclusion. Try to spend time there every day connecting with God.

❧

4   Take some time every day to try and understand the meaning of life. Sincerely seek the answer. God will keep nudging you until you find it.

❧

5   Think back in time and recall an instance when God refused you something you wanted. Can you discern now why God said no?

6  Think of a time when you felt God's guiding hand in your life. What was the message? How did it change you? What is the message that God is sending to you now?

∽

7  List five simple things to do today that would make the world a better place. Choose one and do it.

∽

8  Are there areas in your life where you might be trying to fool God? (This is hard and requires some tough self-examination.)

∽

9  Is there something in your personal development that you are pushing aside? (This requires being really honest with yourself.) What should you do now in order to pre-empt a wake-up call?

❦

# My Favorite Prayers: A Selection

❧

## PSALM 138

I will thank You with all my heart, in the presence
of the mighty will I sing praises to You. I will bend my
knees to Your Holy Sanctuary, and give thanks to
Your Name for Your kindness and for Your truth,
because You have magnified Your word far beyond
Your Name. In the day I called, You answered me;
You uplifted me—You strengthened my soul...

If I walk in the midst of distress You keep me alive.
Against the wrath of my enemies You stretch forth
Your hand, and Your right hand delivers me.
The Lord will accomplish that which concerns me.
Lord, Your kindness endures forever,
The work of Your hands forsake not.

❧

✥

## PSALM 139

Lord, You have searched me and You know me.
You know my sitting down and my rising, You understand
how to draw me near to You from afar. My going about
and my lying down You have surrounded, and all my
ways are familiar to You. For there is yet no word on
my tongue but Lord you know it already...

Where could I go from Your spirit
or where could I flee from Your Presence?
if I would ascend to heaven, You are there;
if I were to make my bed in the grave, You are there.
if I were to take wings of the dawn,
and dwell in the uttermost part of the sea,
even there Your hand would lead me,
and Your right hand would hold me...
Forever I will thank You, for in an
awesome and wondrous way was I formed.

Wonderful are Your works,
and my soul is well aware of this.
My essence was not hidden from You, when I
was made in secret, wrought in the lowest parts.
My unformed substance Your eyes did see,
and in Your book they are all written,
even the days are fashioned; and He
chose for Himself this day from among them.

How precious to me are the thoughts of You,
Almighty; how overwhelming even their beginnings.
If I were to count them, they are more in number
than the sand; were I to reach their end,
I would still be bound up with You...
Search me, Almighty, and know my heart,
try me and know my thoughts.
And see if there be any wrongful way in me,
and lead me in the way of eternity.

≈

❧

PRIESTLY BLESSING
NUMBERS 6:24-27

May the Lord bless you and guard you.
May the Lord shine his countenance
upon you and be gracious to you.
May the Lord turn His countenance
toward you and grant you peace.

❧

❧

## PRAYER FOR DREAMS

Master of the world, I am Yours and my dreams are
Yours. I have dreamed a dream, but I do not know
what it means. May it be Your will, Lord, my God
and the God of my fathers, that all my dreams
regarding myself and regarding all of Israel be
good ones—those I have dreamed about myself,
those I have dreamed about others, and those that
others have dreamed about me. If they are good,
strengthen them, fortify them, make them endure in me...
But if they require healing, heal them...
May You protect me, may You be gracious
to me, may You accept me. Amen.

❧

❧

## BEDTIME BLESSING

May the angel Michael be at my right hand,
May the angel Gabriel be at my left hand,
May the angel Uriel be before me,
May the angel Raphael be behind me.
And may the Presence of the
Almighty be always above me.

❧

❧

## PSALM 23

The Lord is my shepherd, I shall not want.
In lush meadows He lays me down.
Beside tranquil waters He leads me.
He restores my soul. He leads me on paths of
righteousness for his names sake.
Though I walk in the valley of death,
I will fear no evil, for You are with me.
Your rod and Your staff, they comfort me.
You prepare a table before me in full view of my
tormentors. You anoint my head with oil, my cup
overflows. May only goodness and kindness
pursue me all the days of my life and I shall
dwell in the house of the Lord forever.

❧

❧

## PSALM 30

I will exalt You, Lord, for You have upheld me
and not let my foes rejoice over me.

Lord, my God, I cried out to You, and You healed me.
Lord, You have raised my soul from the lower world.
You have kept me alive, lest I descend to the Pit.

Sing to the Lord, His pious ones and
give thanks to His holy name.
For His anger lasts only a moment,
but there is long life in His conciliation.
In the evening one retires weeping,
but in the morning there is a cry of joy!

I said in my serenity, I would never be moved.
But Lord, it was Your will alone that established
my mountain as a stronghold. When you concealed
Your Presence, I was terrified. To You, Lord,
I called, and my Master I beseeched...

Hear me Lord, and be gracious to me,
Lord, be a help to me. You have
turned my mourning into dancing, You
have loosened my sackcloth and supported
me with joy. In order that my soul might
sing to You and not be stilled,
Lord, my God, forever will I thank You.

⧢

## BELOVED OF THE SOUL

Beloved of the soul, merciful Father draw
Your servant to Your will. Then Your servant will
run like a deer; he will bow before Your splendor. To
him, Your affections will be sweeter than the drippings
of the honeycomb and all other pleasant tastes.

Splendid, beautiful, radiance of the world, my
soul is lovesick for You. I beseech You, Almighty,
please, heal her by showing her the pleasantness of
Your radiance. Then she will be strengthened and
healed and she will have everlasting joy.

Ancient One—let Your mercy be aroused, and
please have pity upon Your beloved child;
for it is long that I have yearned
to behold soon the glory of Your strength.
These my heart has desired, please have pity
and do not conceal Yourself.

Reveal Yourself, please and spread over me, my
Beloved, the shelter of Your peace, let the earth be
illuminated from Your glory, we will exult and rejoice
in You. Hasten, show us Your love for the time has
come and be gracious unto us as in the days of old.

❧

## PSALM 27

The Lord is my light and my salvation, whom shall I fear?
The Lord is the strength of my life, of whom shall
I be afraid? When evildoers approach me to
devour my flesh, My tormentors and my foes,
they stumble and fall. If an army should encamp
against me, my heart shall not fear;
If war were to rise against me in this I trust.

One thing I request of the Lord, only this shall
I seek: That I may dwell in the House of the Lord
all the days of my life, to behold the sweetness
of the Lord, to meditate in His sanctuary. For
He will hide me in His Tabernacle on the day
of distress, He will conceal me in the shelter of
His tent, upon a rock He will lift me.

And now my head is raised high above my enemies around me, and I will bring to His tent, offerings accompanied by by trumpets of joy. I will sing and chant to the Lord.

Lord, hear my voice when I call, be gracious to me and answer me. Of You my heart has said 'seek My Presence.' Your Presence, Lord I will seek. Conceal not Yourself from me, do not turn Your servant away in anger. You have been my help; neither cast me off nor abandon me, God of my deliverance. When my father and mother abandon me, the Lord will gather me up.

Lord, teach me Your way and lead me in the path of righteousness... Had I not believed that I would see the goodness of the Lord in the land of the living? Hope to the Lord, be strong and He will give you courage. Hope to the Lord!

❧

## PSALM 121

I will lift my eyes to the mountains: from where will my help come? My help comes from the Lord Maker of heaven and earth. He will not let your foot slip, He will not slumber—your Guardian. Behold, He does not slumber nor does He sleep — the Guardian of Israel! The Lord is your guardian, the Lord is your shelter at your right hand. By day the sun will not hurt you, nor the moon at night. The Lord will guard you from all evil. He will preserve your soul. The Lord will guard your coming and going, from now until forever.

❧